T0113871

Out of the Ordinary

*A mother's reflection of her emotions
on raising a disabled child.*

CATHY TANNER

WESTBOW
PRESS®
A DIVISION OF THOMAS NELSON
& ZONDERVAN

WestBow Press books may be ordered through booksellers or by contacting:

WestBow Press
A Division of Thomas Nelson & Zondervan
1663 Liberty Drive
Bloomington, IN 47403
www.westbowpress.com
844-714-3454

ISBN: 978-1-6642-7813-4 (sc)
ISBN: 978-1-6642-7812-7 (e)

Print information available on the last page.

WestBow Press rev. date: 10/11/2022

Dedication

THIS BOOK IS DEDICATED TO my parents, Jim and Frances. They adopted me into a loving, godly, and beautiful family. My life could have been so different if you had not chosen me as your own. You gave me the foundations to walk through this life with confidence, no matter what comes my way.

Just a Note

I NEVER THOUGHT I WOULD be able to raise a disabled child. I was focused on encouraging those who were strong and healthy. When I was in elementary school, I had the best physical education teacher. She was my inspiration to pursue a career in physical education later in my life. While I was in college, I contemplated becoming a doctor and had the opportunity to work in a veteran's hospital. My job was to wrap the stumps of amputees. This was a difficult job to stomach. The hospital scene was dreary and depressing, and I would rather have worked in a more positive environment. I focused my life on educating people to be healthy and physically fit. I taught at a university for more than thirty-five years in kinesiology.

The birth of my daughter created many challenges to living my life while pursuing a career helping healthy people. Someone referred me to this author's view below of raising a child with a disability not long after my child was born. The life that I lived after my child was born was not what I was expecting. My life has been deeply challenged emotionally, physically, spiritually, and mentally. I hope this collection of thoughts, emotions, and raw views of living in my unexpected country will encourage you, validate you, and remind you that you are not alone in your journey.

Welcome To Holland
by Emily Perl Kingsley
Copyright©1987 by Emily Perl Kingsley.
All rights reserved.
Reprinted by permission of the author.

I am often asked to describe the experience of raising a child with a disability - to try to help people who have not shared that unique experience to understand it, to imagine how it would feel. It's like this……

When you're going to have a baby, it's like planning a fabulous vacation trip - to Italy. You buy a bunch of guidebooks and make your wonderful plans. The Coliseum. The Michelangelo David. The gondolas in Venice. You may learn some handy phrases in Italian. It's all very exciting.

After months of eager anticipation, the day finally arrives. You pack your bags and off you go. Several hours later, the plane lands. The flight attendant comes in and says, "Welcome to Holland."

"Holland?!?" you say. "What do you mean Holland?? I signed up for Italy! I'm supposed to be in Italy. All my life I've dreamed of going to Italy."

But there's been a change in the flight plan. They've landed in Holland and there you must stay.

The important thing is that they haven't taken you to a horrible, disgusting, filthy place, full of pestilence, famine, and disease. It's just a different place.

So you must go out and buy new guidebooks. And you must learn a whole new language. And you will meet a whole new group of people you would never have met.

It's just a different place. It's slower-paced than Italy, less flashy than Italy. But after you've been there for a while and you catch your breath, you look around.... and you begin to notice that Holland has windmills....and Holland has tulips. Holland even has Rembrandts.

But everyone you know is busy coming and going from Italy... and they're all bragging about what a wonderful time they had there. And for the rest of your life, you will say "Yes, that's where I was supposed to go. That's what I had planned."

And the pain of that will never, ever, ever, ever go away... because the loss of that dream is a very very significant loss.

But... if you spend your life mourning the fact that you didn't get to Italy, you may never be free to enjoy the very special, the very lovely things ... about Holland.

Adjustment Is Coming

IT IS EASY TO BELIEVE something that is not true, especially if you want it to be true. When you have a child who is disabled, there are so many things you want to believe that, in the end, are simply not reality. When my daughter was younger, she seemed to fit in with her peers. She seemed to keep up developmentally with what the other children were doing. There did not seem to be much of a gap between her cognitive abilities and the other children. I wanted to believe that having a mentally disabled child was not particularly bad.

As time moved along, the gap between my daughter's abilities and those of the other children began to widen. The same thing happened socially. When my daughter was younger, she was invited to birthday parties, and I even had her schoolmates over for her birthday. As time progressed, the friends grew up and no longer had an interest in my daughter. I therefore had to find other ways to help her socially so she would not be so isolated. The older she got, the more difficult this became.

Unfortunately, parents who continue to believe their child will be like everyone else may end up being disappointed by the truth, appearing unexpectedly and jolting them into reality. The reality you desire is not usually the one you achieve. This is not to say that nothing is achieved. It may just look different than what you originally thought.

Over the course of my daughter's life, I have had to adjust. Some of the adjustments have been easier to make than others. Yet, all were necessary to allow my daughter to become who she is. When you are raising a special needs child, there are goals that are set and norms to reach. However, all the therapists and doctors in the world cannot determine the actual outcome of your child. As you plan for your child and move in certain directions, keep an open mind and heart, because it is the Lord who will establish the path forward.

> The heart of man plans his way, but the Lord establishes his steps.
>
> (Proverbs 16:9, ESV)

All Things Work Together

⁓🦋

AFTER MY DAUGHTER WITH DOWN syndrome was born, I became adamant about two things. The first related to her appearance. I remember driving with my dad and seeing someone with an older child like mine who appeared unkempt. I told my dad this would never happen to my daughter. The second was that I wanted her to find a community where she could thrive.

I would always try to help my daughter look her best throughout the years. I got her haircuts she liked, clothes she wanted to wear, and shoes that she loved. However, finding her a community was not as easy. I tried different play groups to develop friendships. These groups did not unite the way we thought they might. I went the route of facilities that took a daycare approach, but they were not a fit for my daughter. Then I tried having a caregiver take her out to socialize. None of these attempts worked, and my daughter spent much of her time at home, with little socialization.

My husband and I had visited a facility that had a residential program for individuals like my daughter. We would go there every so often to see if we were still interested in her living there. During one of our visitations to the facility, the director told us, "You should not wait until something happens to one of you that will force her into a facility." He said it was better that she go in while we were around and let it become her home. When something happened to us, she would be in a familiar, safe, and secure place. The years passed by, and at various times, I was reminded of his advice.

Our hesitation was primarily waiting for a spot and then how we could financially manage it. The day came when there was an opening. Despite wondering how we could pay for the facility, we took her for placement.

My daughter flourished at this facility. My hope for a community from years ago was realized. Even more importantly, the Lord provided all along for His dear child. I could not make her community happen the way I wanted, but He had the perfect answer waiting for me.

> For I know the plans I have for you, declares
> the Lord, plans to and not to harm you, plans
> to give you hope and future.
> (Jeremiah 29:11, NIV)

Always Different

❧

ONE THING I NOTICED EARLY on in having a disabled child was that my family was different from "normal" families. When my daughter was a young child, the difference was not as noticeable. However, as time went on, things changed dramatically. We were not included in outings arranged by other families. We were rarely asked over for dinner with other families. No one took an interest in hanging out with our family. I was always separating the "normal" family members from the disabled one so they could spend time with other families. Most families did not know how to integrate a special needs child into their activities. This was discouraging, as I was always trying to find ways to change this dynamic. It never happened, and as a family, we were ostracized from gatherings and activities other families were involved in.

It is easy to become bitter at the way other families respond. The knee-jerk reaction is to respond in judgment. The Bible warns us not to be tempted into that response. When we judge others, we are judging ourselves. We do not know why other families do not respond the way we would like, but it is not an excuse to judge them. We do the very same thing in other circumstances. Let the Lord move you through these hurtful circumstances with understanding and trust in His design.

> You, therefore, have no excuse, you who pass judgment on someone else, for at whatever point you judge the other, you are condemning yourself, because you who pass judgment do the same things.
>
> (Romans 2:1, NIV)

A Cheerful Heart

WHEN MY DAUGHTER WITH DOWN syndrome was born, someone tried to comfort me with the words, "They are such cheerful children!" I did not want a "cheerful child" at that time. I wanted a normal child. As my daughter has grown and developed, I began to see ways in which my "cheerful child" challenged my ways of thinking and behaving.

During the Thanksgiving holidays, our family participated in a football game. Everyone played, including my daughter. She was the center for our team and relished every opportunity to hike the ball. I was the quarterback and was concerned about how we were going to win the game. As the game progressed, I noticed major differences in how we viewed the game. We were thinking directly opposite of what we thought was important. It was important for me to move the ball down the field. It was important for her just to be on the field. It was important for me to complete a pass. It was important for her to make sure the quarterback was not hurt while making the pass. It was important for me to use the huddle to communicate the next play. It was important for her to have a huddle every play, to be close in it, and to cheer loudly every time we left it. Somehow, I came away feeling the things that were important to her were really the most important things.

The verse in Proverbs says a cheerful heart has a continual feast. My cheerful-hearted daughter was feasting throughout the game while I was highly focused on winning. Her cheerfulness made a difference in our huddle. It caused everyone to be more lighthearted about the whole event. We came out of the huddle "happy." I am beginning to see that it is all right to have a "cheerful child." I will learn more from her about feasting the rest of my life and come away from my huddle with her a lot happier than when I started.

> All the days of the afflicted are bad, but a cheerful heart has a continual feast.
> (Proverbs 15:15, NASB)

What to Do

❧

WITH A SPECIAL NEEDS CHILD, finding opportunities for socialization get more difficult as time passes. When your child is little, everyone thinks they are cute and you are doing such a good job raising them. People feel great about letting their children play with your child. As time passes, those opportunities become less and less frequent. The children grow up and have lives of their own. They have dreams, careers, and even families. There is no longer the connection that was once there, and they move on. What do you do now?

I was always thinking of different directions I could go to seek out opportunities that could occupy my daughter's time and keep her from being so alone. This brought back a memory of a woman in the grocery store I would observe when I would go shopping. Every time she came to shop, she had an adult Down syndrome daughter with her. I thought to myself, *Is this how life will be with my daughter? Just the two of us and no one else around?* Of course, I had no idea about how these individuals really lived, but the image they portrayed was revealing regarding my own feelings.

Although my daughter was particularly good at occupying herself, years of doing the same thing with only sporadic interruptions were beginning to take a toll on her. She would barely engage with people who came to the house and would just go back to being occupied with her "work." It got to the point where she just lay on the floor in her bedroom as if to say, "I give up and do not know what else to do."

The Lord did provide other opportunities for my daughter. But to find them, it took me getting to the end of my rope, not trying to fix it by myself, and seeking the Lord's direction.

> Two are better than one, because they have a good return for their labor: If either of them falls down, one can help the other up. But pity the one who falls and haws no one to help them up.
>
> (Ecclesiastes 4:9–12, ESV)

Don't Give In

WHAT DO YOU DO WHEN your plans have been blown up? Having a disabled child can disrupt any plans for the future. When my daughter was born, I was planning to have three children. She was the second in line, and so, I had to decide whether I wanted to try for a third child. This was a difficult decision. When I gave birth to my daughter, the odds of having a Down syndrome baby was about one in one thousand. Since I'd already had a Down syndrome baby, my odds increased to one in one hundred. A few people thought I was crazy even to think about having another child, especially facing those odds. I continued to ponder the idea of having another child. However, the more I thought and prayed about it, the more I leaned into the Lord, seeking His perspective. I did not want my fear to be the deciding factor in my decision to try to get pregnant. So my husband and I continued trying for a child and were successful. I was blessed with a beautiful, healthy boy, and I am so thankful I have him now. If I had given in to my fears about my situation, this might not have happened. We can certainly trust God, not our fears, when it comes to these issues. His perfect love will guide our lives in confidence and bring about the result He desires for us.

> Behold, God is my salvation; I will trust, and will not be afraid; for the LORD GOD is my strength and my song, and He has become my salvation.
>
> (Isaiah 12:2, ESV)

Exposed

❧

SOME DAYS ARE IMPOSSIBLE. WE all have times when we are discouraged, challenged, or simply in a bad mood. When we find ourselves in these types of situations, we often try to hide them. I am no different. I like to put on a strong, composed face and act as if nothing is bothering me at all. I can go through an entire day feeling miserable on the inside and appear put together on the outside. There are some days when I am not even aware I am feeling this way.

There is someone in my life who is a truth detector regarding my feelings. No matter how hard I try to hide them, dismiss them, or remain oblivious to them, this person always exposes them. You are probably guessing it is the Lord or my husband, who shows me my inattentiveness, but there is someone else less obvious that He uses. It is my Down syndrome daughter.

My daughter resides at a facility for mentally challenged people. The facility is not too far away and an easy drive out to see her. I always look forward to being with her and talking with her about what she is doing and how her friends are doing. When I arrive at the facility, I check her out, and we usually go out to eat at her favorite place, which is Chick-fil-A, before shopping for something she wants. Depending on how things are going in my life, this will be the truth detector. If there is unsettled business in my spirit, I am toast! My daughter will look deeply into my eyes and ask, "Mom, are you okay?" It is uncanny how many times she has unmasked my feelings with that question.

I am taken aback, and I must readjust my thought process to honestly answer her question. If there is a smidgen of dishonesty, she will instinctively know it. She will come back with a follow-up question: "Are you okay?" At this point in the exchange, I can either be honest or try to placate her. Sometimes, I will answer honestly that I am okay, and other times, I will tell her that it will be okay. She usually accepts my answer but sometimes will come back with the same question to confirm her query.

I think this is true in our relationship with the Holy Spirit. He nudges us daily. Sometimes we are aware of His nudge and we answer or ignore Him. Just like my daughter, He is asking, "Are you okay about this?" It is so easy to pass Him off and ignore the interaction. However, He will come back again to double check, just like my daughter, and ask, "Are you okay?"

Do not quench the Spirit.
(1 Thessalonians 5:19, ESV)

Feelings of Loss

⁓❧

I WALKED OUT OF THE hospital with a baby in my arms, feeling empty-handed. I had lost something in the delivery room I could never regain. My baby had Down syndrome. Sometimes, I mourned the loss of a healthy baby, and sometimes, I became angry. My greatest emotional need, however, was to correct the injustice that had occurred. I reasoned that by having another baby, which was normal in every way, I could rectify the loss I carried in my arms.

Arriving home from the hospital, I told my husband I wanted to adopt a baby immediately. I was adamant. I planned to explore the possibilities using different agencies. My husband attributed this unrealistic outburst to my pain medication in addition to strained emotions. He looked at me tenderly and said, "Don't you think you should wait until this one is older before you start thinking about another one? You already have your hands full."

He was right, but I did not want him to be right. I wanted our family and our lives to be normal.

Over time, I began to understand why I was pressing so hard for another baby. This was such an absurd quest after just delivering my baby girl. I felt empty. I felt cheated. I viewed myself as a failure through this Down syndrome baby. From my limited perspective, I deserved a normal child and normal life, which I failed to deliver.

There will be mothers and fathers walking out of hospitals with a child who was not in their plans, a child not even imagined. They walk out believing they are failures, just as I did, but they are not failures at all. Hopes and aspirations for our children can be shattered in a moment—at birth or farther down the road of life. Those who have been given the responsibility of enduring loss can discover, through God's perspective, that they are winners.

It was only when I allowed my expectations and hopes to die that they grew into righteous hopes and aspirations for my handicapped child. It is difficult letting go of the perceived loss but upon letting that presumption die joy will come.

In making plans to meet the needs of this unique child, she is freed from my expectations, which she never could have attained. She is now free to live her uniquely appointed life, and I too am freed from bitter thoughts of disappointment.

> Truly, truly I say to you, unless a grain of
> wheat falls into the earth and dies, it remains
> alone; but if it dies, it bears much fruit.
> (John 12:24, ESV)

Freedom

THERE IS SOMETHING ABOUT GOING to the beauty salon that unnerves me. When I walk in, I feel very insecure. There is a definite intimidation factor of trying to make you look beautiful that brings out my insecurities. By nature, I like the natural look and do not wear a lot of makeup or fuss with my hair. In the beauty salon, I am out of my element. As a result, I am often uncomfortable.

My daughter is the opposite. When we walk in the door, she walks up to the lady, who always has a baby sitting beside her, and asks if she can hold it. She breezes past the woman to make her grand entrance to the middle of the salon floor. Depending on her mood, she might sing, "Take Me out to the Ball Game," dance to the *Barney* theme ("I love you. You love me. We're a happy family") or just shake hands with everyone at their booths and introduce them to me as she passes. By this time, I am feeling a little shell-shocked by all the attention.

The salon is not the only place this happens. I have been waiting in the post office at Christmastime, when the line is a mile long, when my daughter starts a "let's get acquainted" party. She leaves my side, goes up to others standing in line, and introduces me to everyone. We could be running on the track, with me pushing her in her stroller. As we run by a good-looking male jogger, she'll wave and says, "This is my mommy!" I know the jogger is thinking, *What a way to pick up someone*. I am embarrassed each time this happens, and I wish she wouldn't do this.

However, this consistent barrage of celebrity has taught me several truths. I have learned that my daughter is glad I am her mother. I have learned how not to succumb to my shyness, that it is unavoidable. Best of all, I have learned how to be truly free.

When I watch my daughter move through these situations, I see real freedom. She is not bound by the atmosphere of physical environments. She is neither judgmental nor intimidated by others around her. She does not make herself anxious by comparing herself to others. It does not matter what she wears or whether her actions are appropriate. She is always free to be herself.

How I long for that kind of freedom. I pray the Lord will allow me to understand that type of freedom. He has done this through the law of the Spirit. I am free to be me in the Spirit of the Lord. When the Spirit controls my life, I need not worry about earthly things. He will take away the insecurities of this world if I let Him. It would be wonderful not to fear, worry, compare, or struggle. I am praying to walk in the Spirit and not fulfill the desires of the flesh. One day, I hope to walk someplace, anyplace, with my daughter in full swing and find that, just like her, I am free to be me.

> For the law of the Spirit of life has set you free in Christ Jesus from the law of sin and of death.
>
> (Romans 8:2, ESV)

Keep Going

WE ALL GO THROUGH LIFE at times feeling like we are tested. There are various scenarios that magnify the fact that there are differences in thoughts, feelings, and perceptions of others when relating to a disabled child. Although that was never a big issue for me personally, it became an issue once I had my Down syndrome daughter. I began to realize that there were people who did not understand my situation and preferred not to.

The biggest tests came when I tried to integrate my daughter into everyday activities. This typically resulted from a lack of understanding. My daughter liked to dance and wear frilly ballet outfits, so I enrolled her in a ballet class. I called a place that others recommended. My body began to tighten as I placed the call, fearing my daughter would be turned down. The woman who answered the phone asked if she could help me. I told her I wanted to enroll my daughter in a class. She said that she had openings and began to gather information to register my daughter. I told her my daughter had Down syndrome. She paused and asked if I would mind being placed on hold.

A more serious voice resumed the call, explaining all the positive aspects of my daughter while acknowledging her limitations. I was gracefully turned down, and so, I dutifully called another studio.

I eventually found a studio that was willing to accept the registration and allow my daughter to enroll. There were misunderstandings on both sides. I expected them to realize what my daughter could do, and they expected me to realize what they could not do. We were able to blend these misunderstandings into a design that worked for both of us. It takes faith to accept something one does not totally understand and to pursue when being denied. Many times, we must walk through life believing even while being tested.

> By faith Abraham, when he was tested, offered up Isaac, and he who had received the promises was in the act of offering up his only son.
>
> (Hebrews 11:17, ESV)

Hard Work

AFTER HAVING MY DAUGHTER WITH Down syndrome, I did not realize the amount of work and care that was about to begin. Once I had recovered from her birth, I was instructed to get her into an early intervention class.

My daughter was around a month old when I showed up for the first class. Everyone was nice, but they were also businesslike. A physical therapist set the agenda, and off we went into the rigors of intervention. I followed every instruction, as I wanted my daughter to benefit in any way possible from the exercises that were being demonstrated. Many of the "exercises" were what you would expect, but I found a few to be unusual.

There were two of them that made me think, *If anyone saw me doing this, they would call DHR.* The first exercise was called belly brushes. This is where you slap the baby's belly with quick strokes with the middle three fingers of your hand. It sounded like you were thumping a melon. This was to cause the baby to tighten the abdomen and strengthen the typical hypotonia muscles.

The other exercise was even more exciting! You laid the baby in the middle of a blanket and threw her lightly into the air. This caused her muscles to tighten in an isometric manner as she stiffened the muscles going up into the air. I would close the curtains at my home when I was throwing her into the air for fear of someone not understanding what I was doing and thinking it was child abuse.

All this was only the start of work that went on for years in different forms and fashions to help my daughter develop. I will never know exactly how much all those exercises affected her outcome. Even though there were days I just wanted a break, I would forge ahead, and with the Lord's strength, I did my very best for my child.

> Therefore my beloved brethren, be steadfast, immovable, always abounding in the work of the Lord, knowing that in the Lord your labor is not in vain.
>
> (1 Corinthians 15:58, ESV)

Having a Bad Day

❧

I WAS IN THE RECOVERY room, and I could see the face of my doctor peering in through an open space in the door. I was still lying down flat after having a C-section when my husband moved close to me at head level. He told me that our baby had been born with Down syndrome. I was wheeled upstairs to my hospital room after giving birth and I received a phone call from my sister. She told me that our mother had terminal pancreatic cancer and only had months to live. I lay in my bed exhausted and devastated at the same time. I could not even think.

As people heard the news, there was a steady stream of visitors coming to offer their perspectives. Others sat quietly, but all who came had come to support me. By early evening, the visitors subsided, and later that evening, everyone was gone, and I was alone in my room. I sat there looking at the ceiling, exhausted, confused, and hurting. How can you process something like this after it has just happened to you? I felt a little like Job. No good news came my way that day.

As I lay in the hospital bed, I looked toward the heavens and positioned my body as if I were lying on a cross. I said to the Lord, "This is too much for me to bear. I surrender to you. I surrender everything: a normal baby, my mother, and my life. I cannot control any of this. I cannot do this myself; it is too much." As I lay there, I felt the Lord close to me. I could sense His presence there with me. I said at that moment, "I cast it all to You."

I immediately felt a sense of calm and assurance. Nothing circumstantially changed, but I could breathe by giving the weightiness of the day to Him.

Perhaps you are having a bad day. Nothing is going right. You are exhausted and cannot battle what is coming at you anymore. Let your weakness turn into surrendering. You cannot carry heavy burdens in a weakened state. Good days and bad days are going to occur throughout our lives. How will you manage the bad days? Burdens are made to be carried, not manhandled. Let them be laid at the cross of Christ.

"Surrender to what is. Let go of what was. Have faith in what will be."

> Shall we receive good from God, and shall we not receive evil? In all this Job did not sin with his lips.
>
> (Job 2:10b, ESV)

How Could This Happen?

❧

I LEFT THE PHYSICAL THERAPIST'S office with her words ringing in my ears: "I do not know why she is not walking. It might be something cognitive." I was totally deflated. I had worked for months, performing the exact exercises that the physical therapist had prescribed to strengthen my daughter so she would be able to walk. I had done everything correctly and consistently, but she still was not walking. I just could not understand it. Whenever I had worked hard with her, there were good results, which should have been the case in this situation.

I was so upset and frustrated that I told my husband I needed to get away for a few days just to calm down and get some perspective. He agreed that was a good idea, and I went to the beach for a weekend. It was the best thing I could have done to clear my head. While I was there, it dawned on me why I was so upset. My daughter's performance reflected on my performance. She was not walking because I was doing something wrong. It was not her fault that she was not walking.

It was mine! I had failed. I thought I could control the progress and outcome of my daughter's development.

The words of the physical therapist were a harsh reminder that I was not in control. Often, you want to make something happen for your child and it is not possible. We care so much about them and their well-being that we put pressure on ourselves to make it happen. The Lord reminded me that He is in control of my daughter's life and destiny, not me. After the weekend was over and I returned home, I approached the door, and my daughter walked to the door to greet me.

> Cast all your anxiety on Him because he cares for you.
>
> (1 Peter 5:7, NIV)

Letting Go

HOW MANY TIMES HAVE YOU tried to let go of something and had a tough time doing it? Let us just start with letting go of clothes that you never wear but may wear "one day" or when the piece comes back in style. How difficult was it to let your child go off to school for the first time, or to college, or to the person who vows to love and care for them for the rest of their life? Or the most difficult one of all: letting go of someone you love to death. All these "letting go" experiences are difficult at best and gut-wrenching for the person left with the change.

When my daughter was in her twenties, she had the opportunity to live at an excellent Christian facility for mentally and physically challenged individuals. We had to make a quick decision to accept the opening or wait who knows how long for another opportunity. I was excited! This was the opportunity for which I had prayed! This facility offered my daughter a place to live and to belong within a community of similar people. I quickly accepted the opportunity, but I was not prepared for what I would experience.

We told my daughter that she was going to college just like her brothers and that she would live and work there. She seemed genuinely excited that her day had come to do the very thing her brothers had done. The day came to pack the trailer with her belongings and head to "college." When we arrived, she was welcomed by her "friends," and we were directed to her room. My youngest son went with me to unload the trailer and help me set up her room. Once we finished, we admired how the room had come together. My daughter was so happy. As the day closed, we had to return home.

It was time to let go, and I was not prepared for overwhelming emotions. It seemed we were saying goodbye forever. Things would never be the same after I left to return home. My son, feeling the same emotion, started crying. It is never good to watch a guy cry. As we walked out of her new home, I looked back to see my daughter sitting at the dinner table with a whole host of friends and a big smile on her face. My son and I traveled in silence, then began consoling each other that she was going to be happy; she would have lots of friends and have her own life.

As the days wore on, it became increasingly difficult to realize I had let my daughter go. It was as if my daughter had died. She was not here, none of her things were here, and there was no sound or sense of her presence. I was instructed by the facility to wait a few weeks before seeing or talking to her to give her time to adjust to her new way of life. My heart sank even further every passing day. I began to second guess my decision.

The innate sense of protection begins to take over, and as the protector, you begin to struggle to let go of that responsibility and inclination. You think that you failed and cannot handle it, and so you let it go. The truth is that you opened the pathway to freedom and opportunity for your daughter to flourish when she was fading away internally at home.

The day came when I was able to visit her. It was one of the best mental pictures I have of my daughter. I walked into her room, and she was happy, very talkative, and filled with life. My daughter had found friends, including a best friend. She had significance in working a job and was rewarded for it. She was flourishing, and my dream for a community had materialized.

This experience reminded me that Jesus let go of all that was familiar to Him too. He came to earth and died so that we in our sinfully handicapped state could have a heavenly community with Him and flourish in perfection forevermore.

> Who, though He was God, did not count equality with God a thing to be grasped, but made Himself nothing, taking the form of a servant, being born in likeness of men."
> (Philippians 2:6–8, ESV)

Misdirected Anger

❧

I HOPED IT WOULD NOT happen again. We went back to the pool, one of my children's favorite summer activities—and mine too! The children enjoyed every minute of sun, fun, and friends. Later in the afternoon, it was time to go home. As we gathered our belongings to leave, I noticed two boys whispering and laughing at my daughter. She had her bow from her bathing suit in her mouth, and it was hiking up in the back, exposing her bottom. I glared at the boys and jerked my daughter by the arm, told her to take that dumb bow out of her mouth, and get in the car. I sat in the car, still angry. Driving home, I realized I had made a big mistake.

My daughter was not the one to blame for my outburst. I had just taken the brunt of my anger out on the very person who had been wronged. My thought process probably went something like this: *If you were not a Down syndrome child, this would never have happened, and it is your fault.* My anger had been misdirected, and it can happen when you least expect it.

My daughter could not help who she was, but I could certainly navigate the incident better than reacting with anger.

Sometimes, we are ambushed by our emotions and we respond inappropriately, only to feel shame afterward. When emotions surprise us and lead us to make mistakes, we must remember that the Lord has cleansed us from all unrighteousness.

> Whoever is slow to anger has great understanding, but he who has a quick-tempered exalts folly.
> (Proverbs 14:29, NASB)

My Daughter Is Spiritual Too

❧

AS WE GOT IN THE car, I could tell that my daughter was upset. I tried to talk to her, but it was hard to be consoling. I could not believe we had to go through another traumatic time. She had just been through four minor surgeries in the last five months, and this was to be number five! We had tubes put in the ears, adenoids taken out, and loops put in her tear ducts. Her tongue had been stitched back together after a fall, and now tonsils! My daughter had a fear of the hospitals, and for good reason.

As we were on the way to the hospital, I felt like a traitor. Putting a daughter through more trauma and agony was not what a mother should be doing. But since her birth, our lives had experienced so many different forms of dealing with agony and trauma. We had been through countless therapies, which were not happy events. But like all the things that made her cry, I had to remember that overall, they would help her.

To make things easier while we were waiting, I brought a coloring book, crayons, and her favorite books to read. We waited for a while, and we were called back to another room to draw blood. I held her tightly as they drew it out of her arm. Then marched us down the hall to our waiting area. We settled into our area, which had a hospital bed that my daughter was determined not to sit on. She sat on my lap in the chair in our waiting area. The nurse came in to check her vital signs, then asked me to put on her hospital gown. Christin did not want to put on the robe, knowing that if she did, she would be submitting to surgery again. She put up a fight with forceful words and moves but finally put on the gown. I could feel her shaking in my lap as we waited.

I asked her if she would like to read a book. She said she did. As we read, she began to relax a little. Then she quickly grabbed my hand in alarm. I asked what was wrong. She said, "Mom, let's pray." I was shocked that she knew to ask and delighted to pray with her at the same time. As we prayed for her and the surgery, she again began to relax against my body. As soon as my prayer was over, the anesthesiologist came into the room and took her back to the operating room.

I sat in the chair, marinating in what had just taken place. The fact that my daughter could ask for prayer astounded me. She asked just in time, and no sooner had we finished than the nurse took her to surgery. Perfect timing!

God reminds us that He is the One who opens the eyes and the ears for people to know Him. He will do that for our children. I can never fully understand how my daughter comprehends things due to her having Down syndrome. But I cannot try to limit her in her desire to respond to what she does know and feel. That day in the hospital, I learned that my daughter could respond to God. I should not underestimate what He reveals to her but continue to teach and model in faith and allow Him to open her eyes and her ears.

> The hearing ear and the seeing eye, the Lord
> has made both of them.
>
> (Proverbs 20:12, ESV)

Preparation

❧

IT IS ALWAYS INTERESTING HOW God prepares us for things that will come into our lives. He knew that I was fearful about having a handicapped child. I remember seeing them in a special room when I was in elementary school. They were in a separate room away from the students, and we stayed away from them. I never really understood them and preferred not to have contact with them.

After I married, my husband and I started talking about having children. We decided to start trying to have a baby. One morning, while I was praying about this, I heard a voice say to me, "What if I want to give you a handicapped child?"

I told the Lord I did not want a handicapped child. I told Him I could not manage a handicapped child. No matter how many times I said that, the same question kept surfacing: "What if I want to give you a handicapped child?" I finally relinquished tearfully and said I would accept that if it was His will for me.

When my first child was born, he was perfectly normal, and I forgot about the words I heard that morning. My second pregnancy seemed normal, and the baby was developing well. They scheduled me for a C-section with my second child. Everything went as planned, and when they delivered my child, they immediately took the baby out of the delivery room.

I was under anesthesia and still groggy when my husband came into the recovery room, looking very solemn. He leaned in toward me and said, "The Lord has blessed us with a Down syndrome baby girl."

I looked directly into his eyes and said, "It is the Lord's will."

I had accepted my biggest fear, and the Lord had prepared me to give my will over to Him years ago so that I could at that moment.

We never know what lies ahead for each one of us. However, we do know that the Lord goes before us, smoothing over the rough places. We all carry fears around for one reason or another. No matter what comes your way, the Lord is making preparations so you can handle it.

> The LORD himself goes before you and will be with you; he will never leave you nor forsake you. Do not be afraid; do not be discouraged.
>
> (Deuteronomy 31:18, NIV)

Protection

WHO IS GOING TO PROTECT her when I am not around?

This was always a harrowing thought each time I took my daughter somewhere and had to leave her in someone else's care. I had no idea if others would watch out for her or she would be left to fend for herself. When you have anyone under your care, you become protective. The behavior is even more instinctive if you have someone who cannot protect themselves. I felt this way about my daughter.

My husband instilled the idea of protection into my older son after my daughter was born. He told my son if anyone was being mean to her, he should punch them in the nose, because that is where it hurt the most. He told my son that he should always protect her when he is around.

One day, I had taken my oldest son and my daughter to the park to play. It was a nice fall afternoon, and it felt wonderful to be outside. I was sitting on a bench reading a book while the two of them ran around, exploring all that the park had to offer. After a little while, a woman came up to me and said my son had punched her son in the nose. She was upset and demanded an answer for such behavior.

I called my son over to me and asked him why he had punched the other little boy in the nose. He told me that the boy was poking my daughter with sticks and would not stop after he asked him to do so. He then punched him in the nose to get him away from his sister. The mother of the little boy saw my daughter and was upset at her son for doing such a thing, and the confrontation was over. She chided her young son for pestering someone who was different from himself. She immediately apologized and left the park.

While I did not see what was happening to my daughter, my son did, but he will not always be there to defend her either. What should we do when there are no designated protectors? Unfortunately, we will not always have someone there to protect them. We must therefore trust the Lord to raise up people along the way to look out for them. This is a tremendous trust issue for me because I think I am her best protector. This is an unreal expectation with which I wrestle. I must realize that she belongs to the Lord and that He is her protector.

> Deliver me from my enemies, O God; protect
> me from those who rise up against me.
>
> (Psalm 59:1, ESV)

Reality

MY FIVE-YEAR-OLD DAUGHTER LIVES SPRAWLED out on the grocery store floor. I am encouraging her to get up. People with disapproving looks are walking around us. I pull her to her feet, and yet she allows her body to go limp, falling to the floor again. This is a common occurrence when my daughter gets tired of walking. She decides she has had enough, and it is time for a sit-down strike. This may not seem like appropriate behavior for a five-year-old, but for a person who has Down syndrome, it makes perfect sense. When you are tired, you sit down. I remember this is not normal.

Our daughter has been a part of our family for five years, and the initial shock of having a handicapped child has worn off. I feel as if I have a normal household and normal children until a teacher confronts me after school to tell me that she is having a problem with my daughter taking her clothes off in the gym, or I am at a neighbor's house, and my five-year-old daughter spills her drink, gets down on all fours, and begins to lap up the drink on the floor. Not normal!

Occasionally, I remember that my daughter is not normal. I have grown accustomed to her unique quirks that accompany her syndrome. She seems very normal to me until I find myself in a normal situation into which she does not fit. When I do not think about who my daughter is with her syndrome, I have normal desires and expectations for her. But the truth is things are going to be different with her than with a normal child, no matter how much I accept her.

These realities hit us at various times. When I am trying to sign her up for gymnastics class, I must remember that she is not normal. The same applies when I talk to the teachers about her. When I go to church, I must talk to the nursery workers about having her in their class. When I hire babysitters, I must tell them about how to care for my daughter. I have accepted her, but others will not be able to do that as readily. This can be a painful experience when you are alerted to being aware of their disability. But there is a way for us to deal with these reminders.

When we are reminded to look at the reality of having a disabled child, the outlook can be less than satisfying. The Bible encourages us to look beyond what we know to Him. It reminds us to look at the things we cannot see, the eternal aspects of things.

Do you take the time to do this when reality hits you? It is wonderful to view our children through the eyes of eternity. Christ loves my daughter, and He has a special purpose for her life, just like He has for mine. He wants to use my daughter's life to bring people to Himself and confront them with the issue of imperfection and how to deal with it. Most of all, He wants to make her perfect one day. These are just some of the things that are unseen. But these are some of the reasons that God brought my daughter into the world.

> As we look not to the things that are seen, but to the things which are unseen; for the things which are seen are transient; but the things that are unseen are eternal.
>
> (2 Corinthians 4:18, ESV)

Rejection

❧

ONE OF MY BIGGEST HURDLES with my daughter was feeling rejected. These misunderstandings came up when I was trying to integrate my daughter into various activities. An example was when I tried to enroll my daughter in a ballet class because she liked to dance and was fond of frilly outfits. I called a place that was recommended. My body began to tighten even before the woman answered the phone, in fear that my daughter would be turned down. She named the ballet school and asked if she could help me. I told her I would like to enroll my daughter in a class. She said that was fine and began gathering information to register for the class. I told her that my daughter had Down syndrome. She paused and asked if I could hold. A more serious voice came on the phone, and I began to try to sell my daughter to the person on the other end. I explained to her all the positive aspects of my daughter while acknowledging her limitations. I felt like a salesperson.

The truth is that, as parents of disabled children, we are their salespeople. Another word for this is "advocate." Whether we are their teachers, relatives, or ballet school instructors, it is not always easy to do. Just as in any sale, you must make many calls ending in rejection to get one yes. We know our product better than anyone else. There will be rejections, but there will also be acceptance. Whenever there was rejection due to her disability, I would feel anger and hurt. Letting the anger build will only cause me to become more discontent with my child or the person who rejected them.

Our Savior experienced rejection by His own creation. He did not lash out in anger but instead sacrificed His divine privileges for me. I pray that every time I encounter rejection due to the disability of my child, I will sacrifice my privileges and continue finding the right situation for my daughter.

> He was hated and rejected; his life was filled with sorrow and terrible suffering. No one wanted to look at him. We despised him and said, "He is a nobody!"
>
> (Isaiah 53:3, CEV)

So Annoying!

HAS ANYTHING IN YOUR LIFE happened repeatedly that you found annoying? You try to figure out how to handle it, but eventually, the consistent irritation of the issue wins out, and you must deal with it. Figuring out how to deal with such behavior is difficult. Many times, handicapped individuals become obsessed with something and do not let it go. It is like someone consistently prodding you with a needle. My daughter has done this to me on numerous occasions.

I used to pick up the children from school every afternoon. This usually involved a thirty- to forty-minute drive time, as I had to visit two different schools and wait in the carpool lines. I would pick up my daughter first and then head to the other school. My daughter had decided that she wanted "an itsy-bitsy teeny-weeny dog." She would utter this slogan repeatedly on the way to pick up the other children and then continue saying it all the way to the house.

When this campaign first started, I thought it was cute. However, when it continued for weeks on end, it became very annoying. I became desensitized to it, but the other passengers in the car did not. They wanted me to stop her from repeating this phrase. I finally gave in and bought a little chihuahua. The incessant requests for an itsy-bitsy teeny-weeny dog stopped. My daughter got what she wanted because she was so annoying!

My daughter knew I was the person who could make her request a reality. Often, I do not want to annoy the Lord with my requests and back off of my prayers for them. Annoying can be scriptural and in the end, receive a response. Perhaps we need to annoy the Lord with our prayers. Look what happened for my daughter!

> Then Jesus told his disciples a parable to show them that they should always pray and not give up. He said: "In a certain town there was a judge who neither feared God nor cared what people thought. And there was a widow in that town who kept coming to him with the plea, 'Grant me justice against my adversary.' "For some time he refused. But finally he said to himself, 'Even though I don't fear God or care what people think, yet because this widow keeps bothering me, I will see that she gets justice, so that she won't eventually come and attack me!'" And the Lord said, "Listen to what the unjust judge says. And will not God bring about justice

for his chosen ones, who cry out to him day and night? Will he keep putting them off? I tell you; he will see that they get justice, and quickly. However, when the Son of Man comes, will he find faith on the earth?

(Luke 18:1–8, NIV)

Speak Up

❧

MY SON WAS IN TROUBLE. He had disobeyed our rules for driving the car, and we had called him from his room to come downstairs for a come-to-Jesus moment regarding his actions. My daughter happened to be in the room when he walked in. We proceeded to talk with him about the offense and its consequences. The conversation got heated, and words were spoken with great intensity. My son got upset and began to shed tears and became emotional about the punishment about to be leveled. Yet, as the atmosphere ratcheted up, my daughter came alive. She looked sternly at my husband and me and said, "You stop that!" She looked angry and protective. I was surprised by her response.

I know that I have often thought that my mentally disabled child has no idea of the content of what is happening. However, in this situation, she seemed very in tune with what was happening with her brother. The more forcefully we spoke, the more she interrupted, repeating emphatically, "You stop that. You stop that now!" She continued her scolding, "You are being bad. You stop that!"

When my daughter was younger, I was concerned with how others would treat her when I was not there to protect her. I had evoked a mindset to be protective of her in my sons when they saw something or someone who might harm her. There were times when I saw their protection in action and was so thankful that they would act on behalf of their sister. I never would have dreamt she would think the same way about them! But she did, and she stood up for them when she saw something she perceived as bad happening to them.

My daughter was quick to take up for someone she thought needed support. I wonder whether I would defend someone who was being unfairly treated or taken advantage of. There are shows on television today that reveal people's responses in conflict situations. As we watch to see how they will respond, people often walk by and gawk at the spectacle. I pray that I would speak up with gusto, just like my daughter when she thought someone was suffering.

> Open your mouth for the mute, for the rights of all who are destitute. Open your mouth, judge righteously, defend the rights of the poor and needy.
>
> (Proverbs 31:8–9, ESV)

Stay Alert

SOMETIMES YOU ARE CAUGHT OFF guard. When our children reach adulthood, we begin to think that we have overcome the major hurdles in their lives. However, when my adult child came home from her facility for Thanksgiving and Christmas one year, I noticed a major change in her behavior and began to worry about what was happening to her. This situation reminded me that my supervision of my daughter is never over, even though she is now an adult. She is aging like the rest of us and will continue to need my assistance. I must stay alert and be aware of my daughter's changes and not grow complacent in her care.

It has taken energy and persistence to care for my daughter over the years. As caretakers, we are aging as well and may not be able to maintain our intensity. I must rely on the Lord to give me the energy and strength to do what is necessary for my daughter. I need this same mindset in my own life spiritually. I do not want to become complacent and be caught off guard with sin. I pray that the Lord will give me His power and strength to do both.

> Be watchful and alert, stand,—for you can stand,—in the faith alone, without help; be brave, and master yourselves. Then you will have nothing to fear.
>
> (1 Corinthians 16:13–14, GWC)

Tender Moments of Truth

WHAT COULD BE POSITIVE ABOUT having a child with disabilities? The news program *20/20* was interviewing a father of a Down syndrome child, and he began to cry with joy when he talked about her. He said you needed to have a child like that to understand what he was trying to say. He said that she brought joy to his life. With such difficult paths that all parents of disabled children face, where does the experience of joy come from?

Through my journey with my disabled child, I have discovered the joys embedded in tender moments of truth. It is when things materialize that you never thought would happen. When you find out your child has disabilities, all you can think about are "the nevers." They will never walk, talk, marry, and on and on.

It would take work for these children of different disabilities to do anything that normal children do with unconscious ease. My daughter learned to crawl by a rigorous pattern of movements, which she had to master to make her strong enough to crawl. She cried the whole time as she practiced the movements. I sweated bullets the whole time I made her do it. But she learned to crawl—a proud moment of truth. Each disability we encountered had to be targeted with a prescribed method of action. Each time progress was reached, a "never" was erased, which brought extraordinary joy.

As time goes on, you will see more of these tender moments that bring a unique type of joy to a parent's heart. They are not giant advances or profound accomplishments in the world's eyes. Many times, they are found in a response that you thought could not exist. I was driving my daughter home from school one afternoon, and she began to tell me about her friends at school. Her favorite friend was Becca. She tapped me on the arm and said, "Becca and I are the same!"

I answered, "Oh, really! How are you the same?"

She said, "Jesus!"

She had put together that they both knew about Jesus. At that moment, I thanked God that he had allowed my daughter to understand a small part of His truth.

Your friends and acquaintances may see your child as a burden or a tragedy. These are feelings generated by what people observe. God has a different view. You can share in His view when you encounter these moments of truth. He allows you to see a joy-filled side of this person that many do not experience.

The father was exactly right when he said you had to have a child like that to understand what he was trying to say. There is a whole lot more to your child than meets the eye.

> (1 Samuel 16:7b, ESV) For the Lord sees not as man sees, man looks on the outward appearance, but the Lord looks on the heart.

The Best Explanation

ON OCCASION, PEOPLE WOULD ASK me what it was like having a disabled child. It was hard to describe to someone the entire dynamic of having a disabled family member. They would ask me what she was like and how I dealt with it. So many thoughts that would cascade into my mind that it was hard to accurately come out with a good explanation.

One day, on my way home from school, I picked up my son and some of his friends, then headed to pick up my daughter with Down syndrome at another school. I could hear them talking in the back seat of the car. My son told them we were going to pick up his handicapped sister. One of the boys asked, "What is she like?"

He replied, "She acts like a normal person, but sometimes she is hard to understand, and even though she is ten years old, she may seem like a five-year-old." He said this very matter-of-factly. His friend seemed satisfied with that answer.

When we drove up to the pickup line at the school, she got in the car. She hopped in the back seat with the rest of the children. No one seemed uncomfortable or curious. The boys interacted with my daughter as they would have with anyone else. My son's explanation had put everyone at ease and normalized her presence. He was able to describe his sister in the simplest of terms.

We try to produce all kinds of ways to describe our unique situations. However, the best explanation is made in the simplest terms.

> A person's words can be life-giving water; word of true wisdom are as refreshing as a bubbling brook.
>
> (Proverbs 18:4, Classic NET)

Fulfilling the Law

❧

SIBLINGS PLAY A TREMENDOUS ROLE in the lives of disabled children. The characteristics of each sibling will influence the life of their disabled brother or sister. I often wondered throughout their childhood and adolescent years how my children would relate to each other when they all became adults. My daughter with Down syndrome is sandwiched between two brothers. They both offered unique influences in their relationship with her.

They are all in their thirties now, and I am beginning to see how they will relate to each other as time goes on. My oldest son is a lawyer and seems to be concerned with my daughter's protection and care. His profession segues into the part of my daughter's world where she may need an advocate, and he is the the perfect person to make sure no one takes advantage of her. He is passionate about standing up for those less fortunate and making sure they have what they need.

My younger son is in business. His work is not his passion. He is active and athletic in nature. He has a more obvious compassionate side. He is tenderhearted in the way relates to her. He always saw himself as my daughter's friend growing up, and it remains that way today.

My children are family and will always have an enduring love for each other. I am blessed to watch their relationships mature in their own distinct ways. The whole law will be fulfilled—loving each other.

> For the whole law is fulfilled in one word:
> "You shall love your neighbor as yourself."
> (Galatians 5:14a, ESV)

Them

⤳

I WALKED INTO THE CHURCH looking for a place to sit. Someone reached out and grabbed my arm. Immediately, I became nervous at the thought of having to sit with the one who caught hold of me. These two people were quite different from me. I was not sure if this was going to work. One of them was not too bad. Her body was deformed and twisted, yet she was able to communicate clearly, and we enjoyed a good conversation. The other person was racked by convulsive movements. Her speech was extremely hard to discern, and I labored to understand her. However, being the "good Christian" that I am, I decided to sit down and worship with them. At this point, it was interesting to note my feelings.

I felt a little uncomfortable because I was not in "normal" looking company. I wondered if anyone around me thought differently about me because I was sitting with "them." I decided that it did not matter because Christ would have identified with them.

Throughout the service, I found myself disrupted in my worship because I needed to help one of them open her Bible, open and close her hymn books, put her offering in the offering plate, as well as straining to understand her choppy speech. In fact, it was inconvenient. I was inconvenienced because I had to help them.

I was amazed at the feelings I encountered while sitting with them, mainly because I thought that I had truly accepted the handicapped. After all, I had a handicapped daughter of my own. However, out of my worship with "them," I realized two things. It is not natural in our fallen state to be inconvenienced by the weak. Yet we are exhorted—those who are strong ought to bear the weaknesses of those who are without strength and not just please ourselves.

Those who are handicapped must depend on the strength of others to help them in their daily lives. One of the people I sat with needed my help in the church service. Without me, it would have been a lot more difficult for her to be able to worship. My strength made her life "normal" at that moment. It barely inconvenienced me yet catapulted her much closer into her enjoyment of worshiping her Creator.

Compassion toward them was not an attitude oozing from my soul toward them. It is interesting that Christ thought that compassion was more important than sacrifice. Perhaps He knew that the sacrifice would come through the knowledge of compassion. I realized compassion was the innate attitude of God rather than men. In seeing the glaring physical faults of these individuals, it highlighted my own handicaps. They reminded me of weaknesses that somebody must bear for another person. I did not want to be that someone—look for somebody else. Yet, as I began to focus on Christ's bothersome task of dying for all my handicaps, I was no longer inconvenienced by their weaknesses, and when I was no longer inconvenienced, the "them" became "we."

> Christ says, "I desire mercy and not sacrifice. For I came not to call the righteous, but sinners."
>
> (Matthew 9:12, ESV)

Touch

TODAY, I HAD A VERY important date. It was so important that I arrived half an hour early. As I sat there waiting for the bell to ring, my whole body became a little tense. Today, my daughter was having a friend over. This was not your ordinary friend. This was Austin, a little boyfriend that all the girls in the elementary school thought was so cute. He had wanted to come home and spend the day with my daughter. Today was a big day! As they approached the car, I saw some other girls laugh as they ran by and noticed who he was going home with. But he did not notice, and neither did my daughter. As they got in, I was a little nervous about what to do with them. He acted as though I was not even there and began talking to my daughter. As we drove off out of the carpool line, I watched carefully in my rearview mirror. He seemed very comfortable with my daughter, and they just kept talking. Feeling like I had to make my presence known, I asked if they would like some McDonald's. He turned to my daughter and politely asked if she would like some. There was a resounding "yes!" and we headed for the nearest one.

The McDonald's in my neighborhood is never known for its speedy service, and today was no exception. While we waited in line, I kept a vigilant eye in the rearview mirror. What I saw almost caused me to cry. Austin reached across the seat and during different points while he talked to my daughter, he would affectionately pat and stroke my daughter's arm. He was so tender and patient with her. He looked at her with a winsome friendliness, but the tender way he touched her took my breath away. None of her other friends touched her like that. None showed such sensitive affection toward her.

Touch is such a powerful sense. We all know that. There are times when all of us long for different types of touches. Whether it is a hug, a handshake, a pat, or a stroke, all possess the ability to draw us in, to make us feel secure, to encourage, to strengthen, and to bring healing.

Jesus used touch to perfection. Many were brought to Him for healing.

> Now when the sun was setting, all those who
> had any who were sick with various diseases
> brought them to him; and he laid his hands
> on every one of them, and healed them.
>
> (Luke 4:40, ESV)

He used touch to accent the power of His enlightening words. We see all throughout scripture where Jesus used his touch. He touched a woman who was hemorrhaging, he touched a blind man's eyes and I am sure many others who have not been recorded in scripture. All of them received healing.

Austin reminded me of that power. He brought comfort and joy to me as I watched him accept my daughter through his touch. He touched her the way I would envision Jesus would touch her. Each day, we have the power to do some of the same things that Jesus did through touch. How is your touch?

> And He took them in His arms and began
> blessing them, laying His hands upon them.
> (Mark 10:13–14, 16, ESV)

Weights

I THOUGHT I COULD NOT go any longer. Everything seemed to be going wrong, and none of the ideas I came up with seemed to work. The teachers at the school were helpful for a while, but even with all their expertise, they came back to us looking for answers. My daughter was having behavior problems in school. They came out of nowhere and then got progressively worse. The harder we tried, the worse they became. Behavior modification didn't work, and I dreaded pulling up to the school to pick up my daughter because I knew I was going to get a full report of how "bad" my daughter was that day in school.

Many days, as I made my way winding down the long road into the line to pick up my child, I would think, *Today is going to be different. This will be the start of something good.* Each time, I was disappointed. As the teachers would report to me about the day's account of my daughter's actions, I would sink lower into my seat and just be absorbed in the weight of what the teacher was saying. As I left the school, I felt a heavy weight and burden in response to all that had been reported. I became angry inside at the weight I had to bear. Every step of the way with my daughter had been an extra heavy burden to carry. I wondered when I would just snap under it and why God did not seem to "let up." I complained to the Lord that it was not fair and that this was not the way it was supposed to be. I would struggle before the Lord over my heaviness of heart.

While I was reading Proverbs, a verse stood out with words that answered all my angry questions. "A just balance and scales belong to the Lord; All the weights of the bag are His concern." God was reminding me that He knows what is fair and what is just. I may have my ideas, but He is the One who sets the scales and even distributes the weights in them. He knows when He is tipping the scales and when they are even. Yet every weight that He put on the scale was of concern to Him.

God will add weight to our scales. But every weight will be carefully selected by Him. It is not put on the scale to make us miserable or to give God amusement at our faltering under it. It is put there to adjust the scales to the right balance for our lives. Every weight is a concern and is carefully thought through before it is placed on the scale of our life. Although the weight was not gone in my life, the perception of the weight had changed. I realized that each weight had purpose and added balance to my life. Each weight added kept my life in balance, when I would have regarded it as keeping my life out of balance.

Special children balance out our scale of life. Each incident involved having them continue to balance the scale. Each weight brings more balance instead of less, and as I tip to adjust to the weight, I become more balanced. Our weights can either allow us to stay unadjusted on the scale or bring us to balance. I know I want to come to the middle with every new weight. How about you?

> A just balance and scales belong to the Lord;
> all the weights in the bag are His concern.
> (Proverbs 16:11, ESV)

Who Is Greater?

WE HAD STARTED A BIBLE study for mothers of disabled children. We thought it would be an effective way to get encouragement through the Word of God and opportunities to share the struggles we faced. We had a format of having different mothers lead the Bible study and then open the group for discussion.

During one of our sessions, the group started discussing diverse types of handicaps and how difficult it was to take care of their needs. As the discussion proceeded, one woman in the group said that those with Down syndrome children were "lucky" because they were not as difficult to care for as those who suffered from autism. She went on to say that it was so much harder to find care and good situations for those who had autism. As you can imagine, this was offensive to those who were caring for Down syndrome children. Comparing our situations was not a positive form of encouragement. To prevent feelings from getting out of hand, we closed in prayer and left the issue unresolved.

I always told people that the Lord knew I could not manage very much, and so, He gave me a child that was not severely handicapped. However, after that night, I realized that was the wrong way to think. I needed to realize that everyone's situation is difficult. I have no idea what is going on within someone else's family and the struggles they are facing.

Comparing ourselves with each other on any level only leads to jealousy, quarreling, and bitterness. Let us live the life the Lord has assigned to us with His grace and strength.

> Only let each person lead the life that the Lord has assigned to him, and to which God has called him. This is my rule in all the churches.
>
> (1 Corinthians 7:17, ESV)

Time-Out

❧

I HAVE HAD ENOUGH! WHY did no one warn me how difficult it would be, and why didn't they write a book on how to potty train a Down syndrome child? I was in the middle of uncharted territory. It is hard enough potty training a normal child, but this was a whole new world. I thought we were making progress—and then I opened the basement door. The smell of a bowel movement wafted up the stairs. I descended the staircase only to find paintings of fecal matter all over the walls and various pieces of furniture. I came back upstairs to retrieve a mop and other cleaning utensils.

My oldest son, who was around five years old at the time, was following me into the living room when the culprit (my Down syndrome daughter) came up behind him. I'd had enough. I lost it! I started beating the mop into the ground while my children watched with confused looks on their faces. Seeing their faces, I realized what I was doing. I looked at them and said, "Mommy needs a time out, and she will be back."

I walked to my bedroom, closed the door, and started crying. I told the Lord that I could not take it anymore and asked why He was doing this to me. I told Him I was not built to take care of a child like this one. He knew how I hated to have the job of cleaning the bathroom when I was younger, and this was not the way to rub it in—literally! I walked back out of the bedroom, and two little anxious faces were waiting, peering up at me. I told them that Mommy was fine and that she just needed to go downstairs and clean things up.

Time-outs are effective not only for children but also for adults! Taking the time to vent my emotions and get back on track to be an effective mother was necessary for all of us to maintain a sane life. I am sure the Lord could look at us in the same way. He has had enough of our sin, our ungodliness, and our flippant acknowledgment of Him. This was evident in the Exodus of His people, Israel, and their inclinations to sin. God was ready to rid Himself of such an obstinate people, but He continued to persevere with them. Shall we not do the same with those around us?

> The Lord passed before him and proclaimed, "The Lord, the Lord, a God merciful and gracious, slow to anger, and abounding in steadfast love and faithfulness, keeping steadfast love for thousands,[a] forgiving iniquity and transgression and sin, but who will by no means clear the guilty, visiting the iniquity of the fathers on the children and the children's children, to the third and the fourth generation." And Moses quickly bowed his

head toward the earth and worshiped. And he said, "If now I have found favor in your sight, O Lord, please let the Lord go in the midst of us, for it is a stiff-necked people, and pardon our iniquity and our sin, and take us for your inheritance."

(Exodus 34:6–9, ESV)

You're Not So Special

AS I MADE ANOTHER PASS around the track, she ran out in front of me and said, "I have to ask you this question! Do you think that you are special?" she inquired angrily. I asked what she meant. "I see that you have a Down's baby, and so do I, and everyone comes up to me and says you must be a special person to have a special baby. I'm so sick of hearing that, I could scream!" she huffed. "Why do people try to comfort me with that? I'm no more special than any other parent. In fact, I'm not special at all!" I had to tell her that I had received the same words of comfort, and although I didn't get as mad about it, I also didn't feel that I was any more special than anyone else. In fact, I wished that I wasn't so special!

Since God has given me a "different" individual, he or she is renamed special, and I am renamed along with them. If I were honest with myself, I wished I could shake off the "special" label. I know that I am not so special.

My biggest fear was to have a child that was "special." I never felt the least bit drawn toward "special" individuals, and

I felt uncomfortable being around them. They were always the children in that "special" room at school. Or they were always those "special" people being led around by caretakers to different events. They were the "cute and special" people I would help at the "Special Olympics." But that's about as special as I wanted it to get! I never really viewed them as people. I probably viewed them more on the level of cute people that had the same capacity for life as people's pets. I am being brutally honest, but I want you to see that I was not a special parent and was not fond of these individuals. I was ignorant about them. My view of special people was inaccurate at best! I was not qualified to be a special parent. I have not met any parent who was qualified.

The woman, who angrily approached me on the track with her denial of specialness, was honest and accurate. She was not special, and she did not want to be special. But she had not come to grips with the fact that she now had something that was special. I am still learning every day that I have something special.

My daughter has been teaching me since she was born that she is special and different, and because she is my child, that has made me special and different as well. I have different experiences in life because of her. I also view people like her in a whole different light because I know someone in an intimate way who is special. I have learned that she is just like me—with dreams, aspirations, and joys. With sorrows and fears. She is sensitive to the feelings of other people and can empathize with them in her unique way. She loves me whether I am up or down or sideways. And when the nurse at a checkup gives her a shot and it hurts her, she says she is sorry! How wonderful, and yes, how "special" to have the opportunity to gain insight through someone else's unique view of life.

Yet, I still have my days when I don't like to feel special because *she* is special. That just reminds me that I am not a "special parent." No one is special enough to receive one of these children into our care because most people do not choose to have one of these children. I would rather do what is going to be comfortable and convenient for myself. A child like this is neither of those things. God knew that. He knew that I could never shoulder one of these children alone. But in His understanding, He chose me to do it. He wants to show the world something unique through my child. I have been given the opportunity to help Him do that. If the truth were really known, God uses handicapped parents for special children.

> The Lord looks down from heaven on all mankind to see if there are any who understand, any who seek God, all have turned away, all have become corrupt, there is no one who does good not even one.
>
> (Psalm 14:2–3, NIV)

Not Guilty

I COULD NOT BELIEVE THAT she got out. My daughter had escaped from our vacation house on the beach where we were staying. I thought I had blocked all exits, but somehow, she had gotten out. We were vacationing in a neighborhood-like resort, and she could have been anywhere inside or outside of the resort. I sent my oldest son on his bike to hunt her down, and I took off looking for her on foot. I approached a pond at the back of the resort area and discovered her shoes at the edge of it. My worst fear was that she might have drowned in the pond.

Just as I was pondering what to do next, my son rode up on his bike and said that he had found her! He got off his bike and moved closer to the open door and saw her trying on clothes in a closet, and he got her to come outside with him. I was so grateful that my son found her, and I was upset with myself for letting it happen. Throughout the day, I chastised myself over it. Sometimes, the best-laid plans can be thwarted. I was allowing myself to be held by the shaming process of guilt.

Satan wants to shame us for our inadequacies. No matter how hard you try to ensure everything is correct, you can still fail. Do not let the failure define how you take care of your child. It is just a missed opportunity for success.

> So now there is no condemnation for those
> who belong to Christ Jesus.
>
> (Romans 8:1, NLT)

Printed in the United States
by Baker & Taylor Publisher Services